WYOMING

in words and pictures

BY DENNIS B. FRADIN

ILLUSTRATIONS BY RICHARD WAHL

MAPS BY LEN W. MEENTS

Consultant:
Robert L. Ferguson
Education Consultant
State of Wyoming

CHILDRENS PRESS, CHICAGO

For Elsie and Harold Bloom

Buffalo herd

Library of Congress Cataloging in Publication Data

Fradin, Dennis B.
  Wyoming in words and pictures.

  SUMMARY: Presents a brief history and
description of the Equality State.
  1. Wyoming—Juvenile literature. [1. Wyoming]
I. Wahl, Richard, 1939-   II. Meents, Len W.
III. Title.
F761.3.F7   978.7   79-26511
ISBN 0-516-03950-4

2 3 4 5 6 7 8 9 10 11 12 R 87 86 85 84 83 82 81 80

PICTURE ACKNOWLEDGMENTS:
NATIONAL PARK SERVICE—Cover, 4(W.S. Keller), 34, 43
JAMES P. ROWAN—2, 15(left)
WYOMING TRAVEL COMMISSION—8, 10(right), 11, 12, 16, 18, 19, 2
21, 24, 25, 27, 28, 29, 30, 31, 32, 36, 37, 38, 40
FORT LARAMIE HISTORICAL ASSOCIATION—9
WYOMING STATE ARCHIVES & HISTORICAL DEVELOPMENT—
10(left), 15(right), 42
THE DIVISION OF COMMUNICATIONS SERVICES, UNIVERSITY OF
WYOMING—39
COVER—Devils Tower National Monument

Wyoming

Wyoming (why • OH • ming) comes from an Indian word that means *great plains*. Once, Indians hunted buffalo on the Wyoming plains. Later, cowboys drove cattle into Wyoming. Today, herds of cattle and sheep are raised on Wyoming ranches. Oil, coal, and other minerals come out of the Wyoming ground.

Wyoming is one of the biggest states. But it has no big cities. It has fewer people than any other state. That means there's plenty of room for everyone in Wyoming.

Do you know where ancient Indians placed rocks in the shape of a giant wheel? Do you know where "Old Faithful" shoots water 100 feet high every 65 minutes? Do you know which state first gave women the right to vote? Do you know where there is a city named after the Cheyenne (shy • ANN) Indians? As you will see, the answer to all these questions is — Wyoming.

Millions of years ago there were no people in Wyoming. But there were plenty of dinosaurs. Brontosaurus (bron • to • SORE • iss) was there. Brontosaurus was as big as a house. But it only ate plants. Dinosaurs all died out long ago. Many dinosaur bones have been found at Como Bluff.

For millions of years, volcanoes spat fire high into the air. The ground shook as the Tetons and other mountains were pushed out of the earth. From time to time oceans covered the land. How do scientists know that? Fossils of fish have been found in places that are now dry land.

Teton Mountains

The first people came to Wyoming over 12,000 years ago. They lived in caves. They hunted mammoths. Mammoths looked like big, hairy elephants. Ancient people painted pictures high up on cliffs in Wyoming. These pictures can still be seen today.

Ancient people in Wyoming built the Medicine Wheel. It is made of rocks. Those rocks are placed in the shape of a flat wheel. Why was it built? Some think it shows the sun and the planets. But no one knows for sure.

These early people are thought to be related to the Indians who came later.

In more recent times, at least 12 tribes lived in Wyoming. The Crow Indians were there first. They fought with other Indians who came to live in Wyoming. Other tribes in Wyoming included the Cheyenne, Sioux (SOO), Flathead, Shoshone (sho • SHO • nee), and Arapaho (ah • RAP • a • ho) tribes. The Crow were slowly pushed out by these other tribes.

The Indians in Wyoming hunted the buffalo that roamed the vast prairies. They hunted on horseback with bows and arrows. Wyoming Indians lived in *tepees*—cone-shaped tents made out of animal skins. Tepees were easy to move from place to place as the Indians chased herds of buffalo. Some Indians, like the Crow, grew beans and corn. The Indians had a deep love for their land. They made up stories about how the land and the animals on it were created. The Shoshone and the Arapaho told about how the earth was once covered by water. Remember, Wyoming really *was* once covered by water.

No one knows who the first explorers in Wyoming were. No one knows when they came. In the 1500s and 1600s Spanish explorers may have come into Wyoming. In the 1700s French fur traders may have come to Wyoming.

In 1803 most of what was to become the state of Wyoming was bought by the United States from France. More explorers came. John Colter (COAL • ter) was a fur trapper. In 1807 he came looking for beaver and other furs. Trappers could sell these furs for a lot of money.

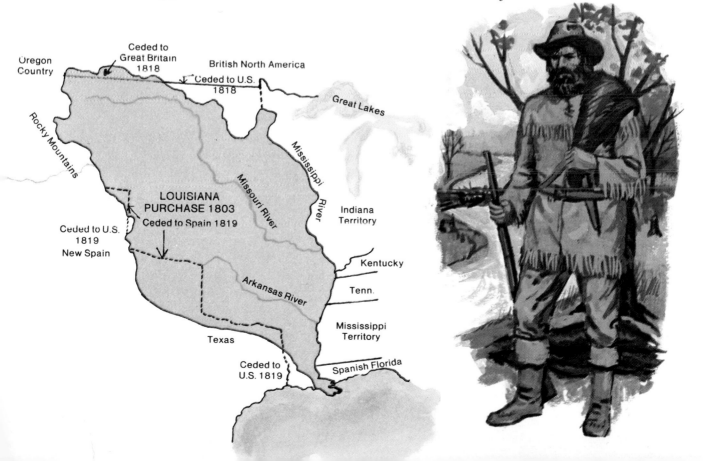

Riverside Geyser,
Yellowstone
National Park

In his travels through Wyoming, Colter met the Crow Indians. They were friendly. Colter also saw the Yellowstone area. He saw its waterfalls and geysers (GUY • zerz) — hot water shooting up from the ground. When John Colter told people what he had seen in Wyoming they laughed. They didn't believe that steam could ever shoot up from the ground. They called the place he described "Colter's Hell."

In 1812 some fur traders, led by Robert Stuart, found a pass through the mountains. This pass was called South Pass.

More and more trappers and traders came to Wyoming. Trappers caught beavers and other animals themselves. Traders got the furs from the Indians. They traded coffee, whiskey, guns, and trinkets to the Indians. In return, the traders got furs worth hundreds of dollars. Indians weren't always friendly to them. Indian arrows ended the lives of many fur traders.

In 1834 two traders built a fort in eastern Wyoming. Their names were William Sublette (SUB • let) and Robert Campbell. The fort they built was first called Fort William. Later the name was changed to Fort Laramie (LAIR • ah • me). This was the first permanent fur-trading post in Wyoming.

Fort Laramie: cavalry barracks

Ruins of 1873 hospital

Left: Jim Bridger
Below: Fort Bridger officers' quarters

Another fort was built in 1843 in the southwest part of Wyoming. It was called Fort Bridger. It was named after the man who built it — Jim Bridger.

Jim Bridger was a hunter and a fur trader. He knew the Wyoming area so well that he served as a guide for many other travelers. Bridger also explored the Yellowstone region. Jim Bridger married Indian women — three times. He lived to be 77 years old.

Parting of the ways on the Oregon Trail

Between 1840 and 1869 droves of people traveled through Wyoming. They weren't coming to Wyoming to live. They were just passing through. The Oregon Trail— and later other trails—went through the South Pass in Wyoming. People were on their way to Oregon to farm. They were on their way to California to look for gold. They came by covered wagon. People on the trails stopped to rest at Forts Laramie and Bridger.

Some fur traders stayed in Wyoming to guide the wagon trains across the land.

Jim Bridger Trek, Evanston

In 1842 the guides Kit Carson and John Frémont
(FREE • mahnt) explored Wyoming for the United States
government. They explored the area of the South Pass,
where the wagon trails went through the mountains.
Frémont convinced the government to build forts along
the trail. More forts were built. Soldiers were sent to
protect the wagon trains in case of attacks by Indians.

The Indians were getting angry. In other places,
settlers had taken Indian lands. The Indians knew that
one day settlers would come to live in Wyoming. Besides,
the pioneers killed many buffalo which the Indians hunted

for food. The Indians also were catching a disease that was new to them. It was smallpox. Before the whites came into the area, Indians didn't get smallpox. Across America, millions of Indians died from smallpox.

The Sioux and the Cheyenne Indians attacked wagon trains. They attacked the soldiers that were guiding the wagon trains through Wyoming. The Indians had some guns at this time. They had gotten them from the fur traders.

In 1854 there was a big fight between United States soldiers and the Sioux Indians. It started over a cow. A settler claimed that a Sioux had stolen his cow. The soldiers went to arrest the Indian. You can imagine how angry the Indians were. Settlers were killing buffalo by the thousands—on Indian land. Now they were coming after an Indian because of one cow. The Sioux chief wouldn't let the soldiers arrest the man.

"If you shoot, all your men will be killed," warned the Indian chief.

"Fire!" said Lieutenant John Grattan, leader of the soldiers. They started shooting. But there were too many Indians. All 30 soldiers were killed.

Fighting continued for years. Indians attacked wagon trains. Soldiers attacked Indian villages. These years were the bloodiest in Wyoming's history.

Some of the Indians were led by Red Cloud, a brave Sioux chief. In 1866, Red Cloud's warriors killed Captain W.J. Fetterman (FET • er • min) and 81 other men in a fight near Fort Phil Kearny (KAR • nee), in northern Wyoming. This is known as the "Fetterman Massacre." One year later, Chief Red Cloud attacked the soldiers near Fort Phil Kearny again. The soldiers used some wagons as protection. They used rapid-fire rifles, too. This time the soldiers won. Hundreds of Indians may have been killed at what is called the "Wagon Box Fight."

Above: Red Cloud
Above left: Monument at the
Fetterman
Massacre Site
Left: Diorama of the Wagon Box
Fight at the Johnson County
Museum

In 1867 there was exciting news in Wyoming. The railroad was coming through. The town of Cheyenne was started when work on the railroad was halted for the winter. As the tracks were laid westward, Laramie and Rock Springs were built. At first, Indians attacked the railroad workers. Finally in 1868 they signed a treaty. Most of their attacks stopped.

Black Hills

In 1868 Wyoming was made into a territory of the United States. It wasn't a state yet. A number of peace treaties were signed at Fort Laramie and Fort Bridger. But these treaties were broken. Indians weren't paid what they were supposed to get for their lands.

Then gold was also found near Wyoming. It was found in 1874 on Indian land in the Black Hills. Miners went into lands where only Indians were allowed. Again, the Indians fought. But there were too many soldiers this time. In 1876 General Ranald Mackenzie (mc • KEN • zee) beat the Cheyenne and Arapaho Indians under Chief Dull Knife in northern Wyoming. That year—1876—the Indian Wars ended. Some Indians went to live on special land, called a *reservation,* in Wyoming. Others were driven out of Wyoming and had to live elsewhere.

In the 1870s and 1880s people started going to Wyoming, instead of through it. They had come to raise cattle. It had once been thought that Wyoming didn't have good grass for cattle. One winter, during a blizzard, a man had to let his cattle loose. People thought the cattle would be dead by spring. But they survived by eating Wyoming grasses. This proved Wyoming was good for raising cattle.

Cattle were driven north from Texas to Wyoming. Giant cattle ranches started. Cowboys did the work. Riding on horses, they drove the cows up from Texas. Cowboys watched over the cattle as they grazed on the grasslands. They rounded up the cattle. Then they branded them, so that people would know which ranch they belonged to. Cowboys also drove the cattle to market, where they would be sold for meat.

Above: Cattle Roundup, Big Horn Mountains
Right: Cattle Branding

Cowboys came from all over. Some were from Mexico. Others were Indian or blacks. Cowboys did carry guns. Most of the time they shot to scare coyotes and mountain lions away from the cattle. But now and then cowboys used their guns on people. If "rustlers" stole cattle, cowboys would go and hunt them down. Many cowboy songs tell of life on the range.

Cheyenne became an important city for the cattle business. Cattle were taken there from nearby ranches, then sent by train to other places. In its early days, Cheyenne was a rough-and-tumble cattle town. Gamblers played cards in the town's saloons. There were hold-ups.

Above: Grecian Bend Saloon, Exchange Bank, and Recorder's Office at South Pass City

Left: South Pass Jail

There were gunfights in the streets. The cemetery, "Boot Hill," was filled with people who weren't quick enough on the draw.

Laramie was also a cattle town. And it was just as wild. Often, the lawmen couldn't do anything about the lawbreakers. In Cheyenne and Laramie, "vigilante" (vij • ih • LAN • tee) groups were formed. They took the law into their own hands. They hanged outlaws. Sometimes they hanged innocent people, too.

South Pass City

Outside the towns, it was even more dangerous.
Outlaws attacked stagecoaches. They took money, mail,
and gold. One place where outlaws liked to hide was called
the Hole-in-the-Wall. In that gap, Butch Cassidy hid his
"Wild Bunch" gang.

In 1883 the oil business started in Wyoming when an oil
well was sunk near Lander. The oil business slowly grew.
The United States government wanted more settlers to
move West. Homestead laws made it possible for families
to get free land. Cowboys bought cattle and started their
own small ranches. Farmers came to raise crops.

State Capitol

Many people felt that if Wyoming became a state there would be more law and order. On July 10, 1890, Wyoming became our 44th state. Cheyenne was made the capital. It was the first state where women could vote. Women had won that right in 1869, when Wyoming was still a territory. Wyoming became known as the *Equality State,* because women could vote there from the beginning.

But there was a fight going on in the new state. The rich cattlemen had formed huge ranches. These "cattle barons" were used to having the whole range for their cattle. But the new homesteaders built smaller ranches.

They fenced off the ranges. Now the cattlemen's huge herds couldn't get to the streams and rivers or get to their old grazing lands.

Fights broke out between the big cattlemen and the small ranchers. In 1889 the big cattlemen had lynched some people—including a woman called "Cattle Kate" whom they said was a rustler. In 1892 the "Johnson County Cattle War" started. The small ranchers had some cattle rustlers among them. The big cattlemen hired some fast guns from Texas for their side. At the KC Ranch, the big cattlemen killed two men. One of them was Nate Champion, who held off over fifty guns for most of the day until he was shot down. Other small ranchers were killed. Finally, an army of the cattle barons met an army of the small ranchers at the TA Ranch, near Buffalo. The ranchers had the forces of the cattlemen surrounded. But before fighting broke out, soldiers came and stopped the battle.

The small ranchers had shown that they wouldn't let themselves be driven out of Wyoming. More small ranchers came. More of the range was fenced.

You can see that the history of early Wyoming is the story of fighting over the land. The Crow Indians had been pushed out by other tribes. The Indians were pushed out by the pioneers. Then the cattle barons fought for the land much like the Indians once had.

Sheep grazing

Later, sheep ranchers came to Wyoming. Once again, there was trouble. The cattlemen said that the sheep used all the good grazing land. In 1909 three sheepmen were killed near Ten Sleep. Again the law stepped in. Some land was marked off for sheep, and some for cattle.

In many areas of Wyoming there wasn't enough water for growing crops. In the early 1900s dams were built. They helped store water. That water was then sent to areas where it was needed. Bringing water to places where it is needed is called *irrigation*. More farmers came.

Oil rigs

In the 1900s, the land yielded more treasures. Oil gushed from the Salt Creek oil field, near Casper (KASS • per). Today, oil comes from many parts of Wyoming. Uranium was found in 1951. Uranium is used as a fuel in nuclear reactors that provide electrical power. Wyoming has become the leading uranium-producing state.

In the 1960s, guided missiles were set up in Wyoming by the United States government. The control center for these guided missiles is near Cheyenne. In the 1970s, a power plant was built in Rock Springs to provide electric power for the state. It was named the Jim Bridger Power Plant. Many other large power plants have also been built.

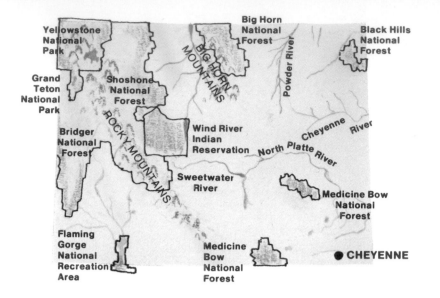

You have learned about some of Wyoming's interesting history. Now it is time for a trip—in words and pictures— through the Equality State.

Yellowstone National Park is a good place to begin your trip through Wyoming. It is mostly in northwest Wyoming, with small parts of the park in Idaho and Montana. Yellowstone was made a national park in 1872. It became the first national park in the United States. It is also the biggest national park in our country.

Yellowstone Lake is one of the largest lakes in Wyoming. Long ago, volcanoes blew a huge hole in the ground. Later, glaciers came and filled that hole. The glaciers melted, leaving the peaceful blue waters of Yellowstone Lake.

Old Faithful

Yellowstone Park has over 200 geysers. Geysers blow off hot water and steam like big tea kettles. Geysers are formed when water seeps down through the earth. Down below, the water hits hot, volcanic rock. The water is heated, then explodes out of the earth. Old Faithful is the most famous geyser in Yellowstone Park. Water bursts up from it about every 65 minutes. The water reaches heights of up to 150 feet. Another geyser, the Giant, has been known to shoot water up to 250 feet into the sky. Geysers don't last forever. Over the years, many geysers have cooled and come to an end.

Yellowstone also has many springs of hot, bubbling water. Grand Prismatic (priz • MAT • ick) Spring is more colorful than a rainbow because of the plants that grow in the water. There are also pools of bubbling mud.

The Yellowstone River flows through a canyon in the park. The rock walls of the canyon are yellow, which is how the Yellowstone area got its name. As the river plunges into the canyon, it creates two waterfalls—the Lower and Upper Falls of the Yellowstone.

Lower Falls of the Yellowstone River

Above: Grizzly bear
Far left: Elk
Left: Moose

You can hike through Yellowstone National Park. Guides will show you around. Be careful, though. There are grizzly bears in the park. Some of them weigh 800 pounds. Elk, deer, moose, buffalo, and black bears enjoy the mountains and lakes of Yellowstone. No hunting is allowed in the park.

Grand Teton National Park is only six miles south of Yellowstone Park. The Tetons are part of the Rocky Mountain system. Many people think the Tetons are the most beautiful mountains in America. Most mountains

Teton Mountains from the Snake River Overlook

have smaller hills around them. The Tetons rise straight up on the western side from the floor of a big valley known as Jackson Hole. The highest of the Tetons— Grand Teton—is 13,770 feet high.

Fossils of sea creatures have been found 10,000 feet up in the Teton Mountains. How could sea life get up that high? Long ago, the Tetons were part of level ground. That ground was covered by ancient seas, with fish and other sea creatures. About 10 million years ago the earth shook. The Tetons were pushed up out of the earth and with them the fossils of sea creatures. To this day there are often earthquakes in the Tetons. And the mountains are still slowly rising from the earth.

Besides mountains, Grand Teton National Park has beautiful lakes such as Jackson Lake. Moose, deer, bears, and elk live in this area.

About a hundred years ago, the Jackson Hole area was home to outlaws. Today in the nearby town of Jackson the days of outlaws are relived in a stagecoach robbery acted out every summer night. In winter thousands of skiers come to ski in the area.

Above: Jackson's South Pass in 1870
Left: Skiing at Jackson Hole

Above: Jackson Hole trail ride
Right: Buffalo Bill Historical Center, Cody

Going north and east from Grand Teton National Park
you'll pass some interesting places. Cody is named for
"Buffalo Bill" Cody, who helped found the town. Cody
was a rider on the Pony Express which delivered mail.
When he was only 15 years old, Cody rode 322 miles
through Wyoming on one trip for the Pony Express. He
also became a noted buffalo hunter while the railroad was
being built.

Today, people like to go to "dude ranches" in the area
of Cody and Sheridan, to the east. Sheridan is the biggest
city in northern Wyoming. At dude ranches, people can
live the cowboy life for a while. They dress in cowboy
clothes, ride horses, and sleep in bunkhouses.

Not far from Sheridan is the TA ranch, where the "Johnson County Cattle War" ended. Fort Phil Kearny, where the "Wagon Box Fight" took place, is also near Sheridan. The ancient Medicine Wheel is also nearby.

As you travel across the northern part of Wyoming, you'll see many cattle and sheep ranches. You'll also see some farms. Wyoming doesn't have much farming, compared to other states. Sugar beets, beans, and wheat are important crops.

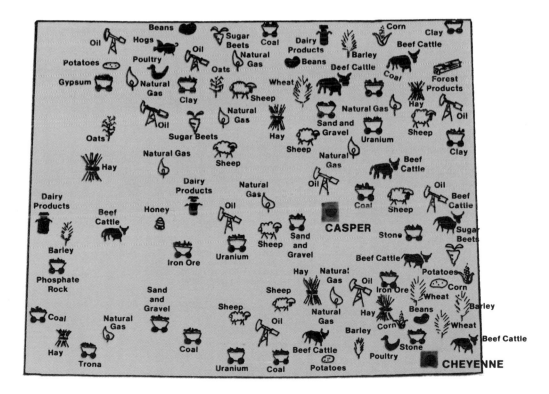

Devils Tower

Near the northeast corner of Wyoming you'll see a strange sight. It is a rock called Devils Tower. Millions of years ago volcanoes erupted, squeezing this rock 865 feet into the air. The Sioux told a story about this rock. They said that once three Indian girls were picking flowers. They were chased by bears. The girls climbed a rock to

escape. But the bears came after them. The Great Spirit
felt sorry for the girls and raised the rock high into the
sky. The bears chased the girls. They left their scratch
marks on the side of the rock. Finally, the bears fell off.
The girls escaped by making their flowers into a rope.

Wyoming has no really big cities. Many of its towns are
small, with just a few stores and a couple of streets. The
names of the towns remind you of Indian and frontier
days: Medicine Bow, Donkey Creek, Lost Cabin, Saddle
String, Skull Creek, Spotted Horse, and Wildcat.

You'll also see "ghost towns" in Wyoming. No one lives
in these towns any more. When miners came to Wyoming,
towns sprang up. The miners left. The towns became
"ghost towns" with buildings but no people. Also, railroad
workers built small towns. They finished the railroad.
Then they left, too. Miner's Delight, Donkey Town, and
Antelope are three of the ghost towns in Wyoming.

Open pit coal mine, Gillette

Coal mining is still "big business" in Wyoming. Coal mines are located at Kemmerer, outside Sheridan, and in the Powder River Basin. Gillette is the center of the world's largest coal mines.

You are heading south towards the city of Cheyenne. But before you get there stop at Fort Laramie. It has been rebuilt to look like it did over 100 years ago.

The biggest cities in Wyoming are in the southern part of the state, along the path of the Union Pacific Railroad. Cheyenne, the capital of Wyoming, is near the southeast corner. Cheyenne is Wyoming's largest city.

Visit Warren Air Force Base, near Cheyenne. The control center for a large number of guided missiles is at the base.

Today, many of the people of Cheyenne work for the state government. Others work at the Air Force Base. Still others work in the oil refinery. There are many sheep and cattle ranches nearby. But during Frontier Days almost everyone puts on cowboy hats as they remember the days of their grandparents. There are Indian dances. There are parades. And there is a giant rodeo. Thousands of people from all over the world go to Cheyenne during Frontier Days.

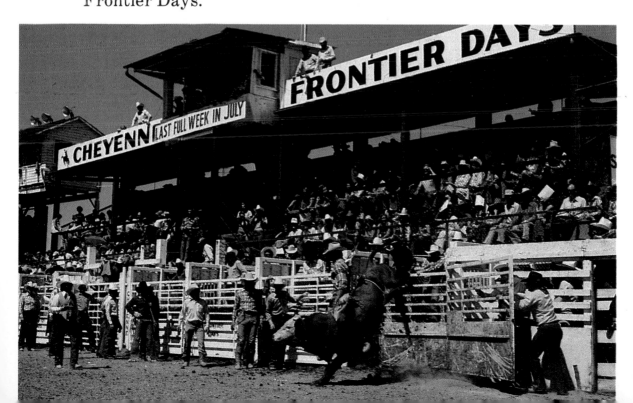

Wyoming Indians

Cheyenne also has some interesting museums. You can learn about the old days at the Cheyenne Frontier Days Old West Museum or the Wyoming State Museum.

Laramie is only about 50 miles northwest of Cheyenne. Like Cheyenne, Laramie was built as the railroad tracks went westward. Laramie was founded in 1868. The town was named after a fur trapper who had been killed by Indians. Don't confuse Laramie with Fort Laramie. They are two separate places named after the same man.

Laramie, too, was lawless at first. In time Laramie settled down. It became a city where ranchers sent their cows and sheep to be sent by train to other places. Today, cattle and sheep are still shipped from Laramie.

Old Main, first building on the University of Wyoming campus

The University of Wyoming is in Laramie. Students from all over study at this school.

Wyoming was the first place to allow women to vote. In 1871, "Grandma" Swain became the first American woman to vote in a general election. She lived in Laramie.

The Geological Museum is in Laramie. There you can see huge models of brontosaurus and other dinosaurs.

Dinosaur bones have been found in Wyoming. On the way to Casper you will pass Como Bluff. There, many dinosaur fossils have been found.

Farming in North Platte Valley

Casper is about 115 miles northwest of Laramie. Casper is the second biggest city in Wyoming. It is near the middle of the state, on the North Platte River. The city was named after Caspar W. Collins, a soldier. Someone spelled his name wrong. The city has been spelled C-a-s-p-e-r ever since.

Visit Fort Caspar. It has been rebuilt to look like it did when Caspar Collins was killed fighting the Sioux and the Cheyenne. The fort, too, was named for him.

Casper is in a big mining area. Uranium is mined in the area. Oil and natural gas are found nearby. These products are shipped from Casper to other places in the United States and the world.

Rock Springs is near the southwest corner of the state. Ranching and farming are done in the area. Oil and gas and other minerals are found nearby.

Fossil Butte National Monument is west of Rock Springs. You can see fossils of fish that lived here over 50 million years ago. Alligator fossils were found here, too.

Places can't tell the whole story about Wyoming. Many interesting people have lived in the Equality State.

Nellie Tayloe Ross (1876-1977) lived in Wyoming much of her life. In 1924 she was elected governor of Wyoming. She became the first woman governor in the United States. Later, she became head of the United States mint. That is the place where our country makes coins.

Francis E. Warren (1844-1929) was the first governor of Wyoming, in 1890. Then he was a senator from Wyoming for almost 40 years. He helped develop the sheep industry in the state. He also worked for irrigation projects. Much of the farming in Wyoming today exists because of his efforts.

Chief Washakie

Washakie (WASH • ah • kee) was chief of the Shoshone. Washakie was a strong warrior. But when white settlers came, he did not fight them. He helped the pioneers on the Oregon Trail. He also served as an army scout during the last Indian fighting in Wyoming, in 1876. He was almost eighty years old at the time. Chief Washakie helped his people get the land called the Wind River Indian Reservation. There, Shoshone and Arapaho Indians live today. Chief Washakie is buried there. The old chief was over a hundred years old when he died, in 1900. He had seen great changes in Wyoming. He had been there when it was an Indian hunting ground. He had seen the settlers come, and then the soldiers. He had watched the railroad come through. And he had seen Wyoming become a state.

Teton Mountains

Home to Indians . . . then fur trappers . . . then cattlemen . . .

Land where John Colter and Jim Bridger explored . . .

Land of Yellowstone . . . the Teton Mountains . . . Devils Tower . . .

The state where women first voted . . .

Famous for such cowboy towns as Cheyenne and Laramie . . .

A coal- and uranium-producing state . . .

This is Wyoming—the Equality State.

Facts About WYOMING

Area—97,914 square miles (9th biggest state)

Greatest Distance North to South—275 miles

Greatest Distance East to West—365 miles

Borders—Montana on the north; South Dakota and Nebraska on the east;
Colorado and Utah on the south; Utah, Idaho, and Montana on the west

Highest Point—13,804 feet above sea level (Gannett Peak)

Lowest Point—3,100 feet above sea level (Belle Fourche River)

Hottest Recorded Temperature—114° (at Basin on July 12, 1900)

Coldest Recorded Temperature—Minus 63° (at Moran on February 9, 1933)

Statehood—Our 44th state, on July 10th, 1890

Origin of Name Wyoming—From a Delaware Indian word meaning *great plains*

Capital—Cheyenne

Counties—23

U.S. Senators—2

U.S. Representatives—1

Electoral Votes—3

State Senators—30

State Representatives—62

State Song—"Wyoming," by Charles E. Winter and G.E. Knapp

State Motto—*Equal Rights*

Nicknames—Equality State, Wonderful Wyoming, Sagebrush State, Big
Wyoming

State Seal—Adopted in 1893

State Flag—Adopted in 1917

State Flower—Indian paintbrush

State Bird—Meadow lark

State Tree—Cottonwood

State Gemstone—Jade

State Insignia—Bucking horse

University—University of Wyoming

Some Rivers—Yellowstone, Green, Snake, Cheyenne, Niobrara, North Platte,
Clarks Fork, Bighorn, Tongue, Wind, Powder, Little Missouri

Indian Reservation—Wind River Reservation

National Forests—10

National Parks—Yellowstone and Grand Teton National Parks

National Monuments—Devils Tower and Fossil Butte National Monuments

Some Lakes—Yellowstone, Jackson, Fremont, Shoshone

Some Waterfalls—Lower and Upper Falls of Yellowstone

Mountain Ranges—Laramie Range, Bighorn Mountains, Medicine Bow
Mountains, Absaroka Range, Teton Range (all part of Rocky Mountains)

Farm Products—Beef cattle, sheep, milk, eggs, sugar beets, wheat, beans

Fishing—Trout, walleye, bass, crappie, perch, catfish, bluegill

Wildlife—Pronghorn antelopes, elk, mule deer, white-tailed deer, moose, mountain sheep, grizzly bears, black bears, mountain lions, badgers, foxes, ducks, geese, pheasants, bald eagles, golden eagles, prairie dogs

Mining—Uranium, oil, natural gas, coal

Manufactured Products—Food products, coal products, oil products, wood products

Population—374,000 (1975 estimate)

Major Cities—Cheyenne 49,600
          Casper 45,800
          Laramie 26,000
          Rock Springs 20,700
          Sheridan 13,200

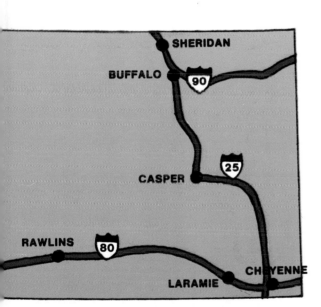

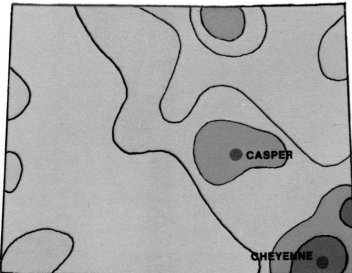

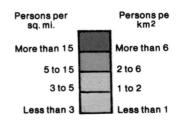

Persons per sq. mi.	Persons per km2
More than 15	More than 6
5 to 15	2 to 6
3 to 5	1 to 2
Less than 3	Less than 1

45

Wyoming's History

There were people in Wyoming at least 12,000 years ago, probably much longer

1743—The Vérendrye brothers, French traders, view Bighorn Mountains and possibly enter Wyoming

1803—By Louisiana Purchase, Wyoming becomes part of United States

1807—John Colter becomes first white explorer known to enter Wyoming

1812—Robert Stuart finds South Pass through Rocky Mountains

1830—Kit Carson is in Wyoming

1832—Captain Benjamin Bonneville leads first wagons through South Pass; also finds oil in Wyoming

1834—Fort William (later Fort Laramie) is founded

1842—John Frémont explores Wyoming with Kit Carson

1843—Jim Bridger builds Fort Bridger

1846—Congress votes to build forts on Oregon Trail

1847—Mormons cross Wyoming

1854—Indians kill about 30 U.S. soldiers in "Grattan Massacre"

1865—Caspar Collins dies in Battle of Platte Bridge

1866—Indians, fighting for their lands, kill 82 in "Fetterman Massacre"

1867—Cheyenne is founded

1868—Big year in Wyoming! Territory of Wyoming is created; treaty creates Wind River Indian Reservation; Laramie is founded

1869—Women get right to vote; railroad is completed across Wyoming

1870—People begin to homestead in Wyoming Territory and population reaches 9,118

1872—Yellowstone becomes our first national park

1876—Indian fighting ends in Wyoming

1883—First oil well in Wyoming is drilled near Lander

1885—About 30 Chinese people are killed in riot at Rock Springs

1886—Terrible winter kills thousands of cattle

1887—University of Wyoming opens in Laramie

1890—On July 10 Wyoming becomes our 44th state!

1892—"Johnson County Cattle War"

1895—An oil refinery is built at Casper, helping city grow

1897—First Cheyenne Frontier Days is held

1900—92,531 people live in state of Wyoming; Chief Washakie dies

1902—J.C. Penney opens his first store—in Kemmerer, Wyoming

1906—First National Monument in United States, Devils Tower National Monument, is created

1910—Shoshone Dam is completed (now called Buffalo Bill Dam)

1914-1918—During World War I, 11,393 Wyoming people are in uniform

1924—Nellie Tayloe Ross is first woman elected governor of a state

1929—Grand Teton National Park is created

1933—Nellie Ross becomes first woman director of U.S. Mint

1947—F.E. Warren Air Force Base is formed near Cheyenne

1951—Big uranium find is made in Wyoming

1959—Earthquake hits Yellowstone National Park

1960—Guided missiles are set up in Wyoming with control center at Warren
Air Force Base

1965—Happy 75th birthday, Equality State!

1972—Coal and oil mining are becoming big businesses

1974—Jim Bridger Power Plant opens in Rock Springs

1975—Edward J. Herschler begins term as governor

1978—Wyoming booming with growing energy industries

INDEX

47

INDEX, Cont'd.

About the Author:

Dennis Fradin attended Northwestern University on a creative writing scholarship and graduated in 1967. While still at Northwestern, he published his first stories in *Ingenue* magazine and also won a prize in *Seventeen's* short story competition. A prolific writer, Dennis Fradin has been regularly publishing stories in such diverse places as *The Saturday Evening Post, Scholastic, National Humane Review, Midwest,* and *The Teaching Paper.* He has also scripted several educational films. Since 1970 he has taught second grade reading in a Chicago school—a rewarding job, which, the author says, "provides a captive audience on whom I test my children's stories." Married and the father of three children, Dennis Fradin spends his free time with his family or playing a myriad of sports and games with his childhood chums.

About the Artists:

Len Meents studied painting and drawing at Southern Illinois University and after graduation in 1969 he moved to Chicago. Mr. Meents works full time as a painter and illustrator. He and his wife and child currently make their home in LaGrange, Illinois.

Richard Wahl, graduate of the Art Center College of Design in Los Angeles, has illustrated a number of magazine articles and booklets. He is a skilled artist and photographer who advocates realistic interpretations of his subjects. He lives with his wife and two sons in Libertyville, Illinois.

DATE DUE